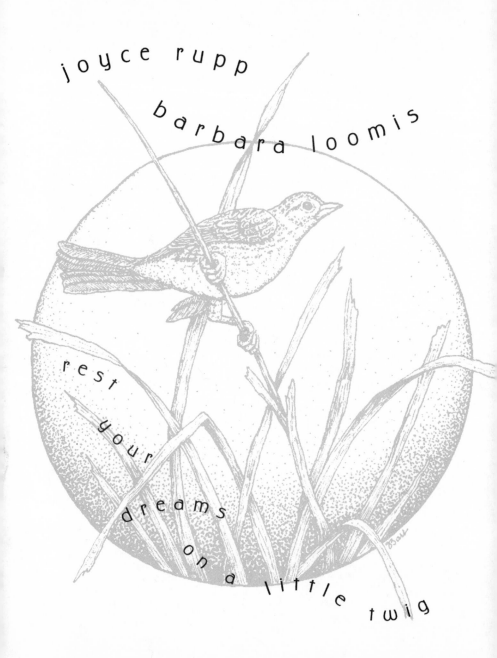

joyce rupp

barbara loomis

rest

your

dreams

on a little twig

joyce rupp
barbara loomis

rest your dreams on a little twig

Sorin Books   Notre Dame, Indiana

© 2003 text by Joyce Rupp, OSM, art by Barbara Loomis, OSM

www.sorinbooks.com

International Standard Book Number: 1-893732-57-6

Cover and text design by K. H. Coney

Printed and bound in the United States of America.

Library of Congress Cataloging-in-Publication Data
Rupp, Joyce.
    Rest your dreams on a little twig / poetry by Joyce Rupp ; art
by Barb Loomis.
        p. cm.
    ISBN 1-893732-57-6
    1. Nature--Poetry. 2. Religious poetry, American. I. Title.
PS3618.U64 R47 2003
811'.6--dc21

                                                    2002014556

To my mother, Ann Loomis,
my sister, Bev Job,
and in memory of my father,
William (Bill) Loomis

Barb Loomis

To the created world,
source of inspiration
for these poems,
and to Divine Mystery,
who continually draws me
to see the deeper things of life

Joyce Rupp

Contents

Acknowledgments. 9

Introduction 10

Dreams of Growth. 12

Dreams of Inner Freedom 58

Dreams of Peace 102

A Note From the Artist 149

Acknowledgments

A heartfelt thank-you to my family, friends, Servite community, and artist-friend-mentors, especially Joyce Rupp, who have encouraged me and/or given me the opportunity to make art my ministry. Each of you is in my heart and known to our generous and loving God. Thank you for gracing and gifting my life.

—Barb Loomis

Many of these poems were written while I was a guest of the Benedictine Sisters of St. Walburga in Colorado; how grateful I am for their gracious hospitality. Mary F. Kunkel's birthday gift to me years ago motivated me to contemplate nature. Many people have encouraged and called forth the poet in me—what a gift each has been! Barb Loomis gave the poems shape and visual expression. Her illustrations are a feast for my eyes and heart. My life as a writer has been enlivened and sustained by faithful and faith-filled supporters, particularly Janet Barnes and Dorothy Sullivan. And a note of great thanks goes also to Sorin Books for believing in Barb's art and my poetry.

—Joyce Rupp

Introduction

Nature is always teaching me. When I pause amid my busy, crowded days and allow my contemplative spirit to settle into solitude and stillness, I am amazed at what I learn. Dreams waiting to be heard rise up in me as I keep company with Earth and her vast array of creatures and elements. They challenge me toward greater transformation, woo me toward deeper wisdom, and set my soul singing with the hope of fuller inner freedom.

The poems in this collection began as little sketches of inspiration. While I observed birds, plants, animals, trees, insects, water, and other marvels of our planet, I experienced a sense of something present that was more than just an external awareness. Being with these simple gifts of creation in an attentive way drew me into a mystical world where words were sparse but wisdom was pervasive.

In pondering nature, I gradually moved from my small space of self into another world of existence. As I did so, I noticed a vital kinship stretching between this existence and mine. It eventually drew me back toward my life again. I saw how each bluebird, mushroom, and frog had a history, a "personality," and a pattern of growth. In seeing this, I was then led to find a connection with my own pattern of growth. I saw how parts of my inner story were reflected in nature: wildflowers swaying in the breeze and little birds winging their way in the wide sky drew me to recognize the caged places of my own spirit. The aged frame of an old tree beckoned to my ongoing struggle with aging and bodily demise. A brown, speckled sparrow sitting trustingly on a tiny twig taught me to have confidence in the fragments of my future until they were able to gather and take shape. A tall evergreen tree encouraged me to believe in my ability to endure.

It was with these sixty-five poetic sketches that I approached Barb Loomis one day. I plopped them on her desk and suggested she take a look at them to see if she would want to create an illustration to accompany each one. Now that I look back at that moment, I am astounded at Barb's positive and enthusiastic response. She readily and graciously agreed to the project and now, two years later, the poems and the illustrations have come together. We offer them to you with hope that these dreams of growth, freedom, and peace will dance into your own story of life and lead you to places deep within your soul.

Joyce Rupp

dreams of

growth

It doesn't take much
to hold the tiny weight
of a song sparrow,
any little twig will do,
or a sturdy weed in a field.

Why do I think my fledgling ideas
have to wait for a thick branch
or a secure landing place
before I set them down?

The wisp of a fleeting dream
can rest for a while
on a small extension in my soul.

If I never let these dreams land,
they will not gain strength
for the long flight into fullness.

All it takes is a little twig
to rest a great dream on.

The old owl
rests in her home,
waiting for night
to seek nourishment.

Is that what needs
changing
in my life?

I keep expecting
daylight to feed me.
Maybe I, too,
need to fly in the night,
wing through dark woods,
seeking inner nourishment.

I will rest
like an old owl,
and go seeking
food for my soul
in the long nights
of silence.

Spring flowers
preach the gospel:
we who have died
are alive today.

We who risked winter
now raise our heads high
to the glorious sun.

Delicate petals,
daughters of resilience,
they call to me,
encouraging the heart
of true believing.

Swallows
swoop down
catch
lift up
swoop down
catch
lift up.

This simple pattern
of nourishment
echoes
the feeding
of my soul.

I get scared
of the downward
swoops,
want only the
lifting up

but the swallow
in me
knows better,
and continues
to swoop down
catch
lift up.

The loveliness
of a single flower
in radiant bloom
can sing
my drooping spirit
into joy.

The loveliness
of a single person
with a listening gaze
can sing
my heavy heart
back into life.

I've come across
both kinds
in my time of need

and both
have brought me hope.

Help!
I've just been born
and I am not so sure
I like this cold world.

Where is my warmth?
Where is my food?
Who will give me shelter?
I do not like this
insecurity and discomfort
thrust upon me.

The voice of a newborn
in the woods
echoes in every challenge
I experience,
in every life moment
when I am called
to change, to grow.

Quiet as the slipping
of the red orb into sunset,
unobtrusive as the first star
shining in the evening sky,
so the young ducks
slide across the silent pond.

I do not see
their yellow-webbed oars
swiftly moving
beneath their bodies,
carrying them contentedly
upon the green water.

Two young ducks
reach the other shore,
beckoning my webfootedness
to do its part as well.

What is it in me
that believes I can move
across the waters of my life
without using
my spiritual oars?

What passive stranger
continues to urge my spirit
toward a lack of intention?

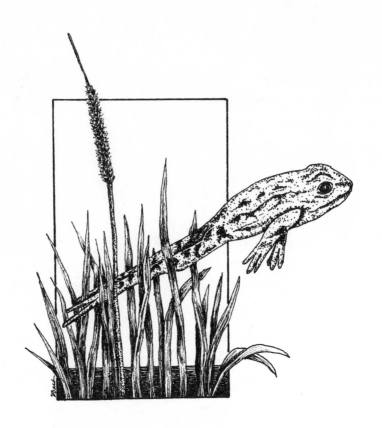

A leaping frog,
transfigured in form
from unassuming tadpole,
tantalizes my search
for transformation.

Trust the ordinary,
take heart, be patient,
be willing to stretch
into unknown transition.

I still look for easy growth
and instant change,

when all the while
frog legs and happy croaks
are gestating within me.

Flowers last
a long, long time
if they have
what they need.

Why is it
that I neglect
myself?

I need to feed
on beauty,
walk more often
under starlight,
listen to the wind,
and rest my weariness.

Then my flowers
will last
a long, long time.

Evergreen,
silent sentinel of hope
through all seasons.

Somewhere
deep within me
an evergreen grows,
strong, tall, resilient,
always singing
of life.

Her stouthearted green
endures, thrives
amid winter wilds.

She is strong.
She is evergreen.
She lives in me.

If only
we could be
more patient,
more hopeful,
more trusting
with the snail-part
of ourselves.

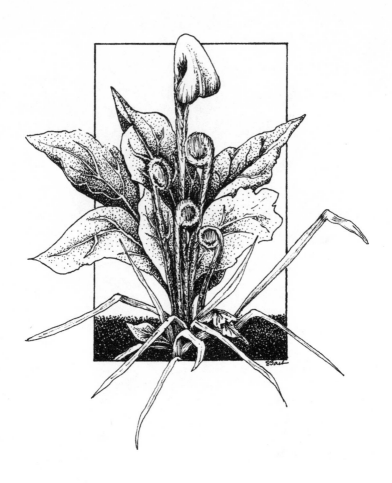

The fern unfolds
slowly,
surely.

Life unfolds
slowly,
surely.

I grow impatient,
want meaning,
NOW.

I seek growth
but seek it fully,
forgetting
that I am the fern
unfolding
slowly,
surely.

The constant rainfalls of May
have drenched its flowers.
Petals lovely in sunlight
are submerged in puddles.

I waited long through winter
for the joy of blooming things,
now only to see them crushed
under weight of unwanted weather.

Perhaps the flowers I seek
must be the deeper ones
that live on in the heart,
where winter snows
do not fall out of season
and harsh raindrops
do not destroy blooming.

But, ah, even there in the heart
the winter weather is unstable.

Negative emotions,
small munching creatures
eating away at the green,
devouring
the life-giving energy.

Negative emotions
chomp off life,
leaving me
a stripped stem
of discontent.

Negative emotions,
catch them
before they take hold
and destroy
the whole plant.

Dragonfly,
do your thin, transparent wings
hold genetic secrets
of fiery-breath creatures
flying the skies eons ago?

Dragonfly,
as you flit among the grasses,
do you sometimes
sense a strange longing
to be at home
in another time?

Dragonfly,
can you tell me
what this strange yearning
might be
that rises up within me
when I taste sunrises
and hear the melody
of stars?

A green shoot grows
out of an old tree stump,
announcing to the world
that power lies within death.

All the resurrections
ever birthed in this world
find a sister
in this green shoot growing
from the old wooden stump.

Things in me that have died,
the worn-out and the worthless,
they are waiting to give rise
to some green shoot
of a sister.

They are inviting me
to faith in resurrection
and reverence
for old tree stumps.

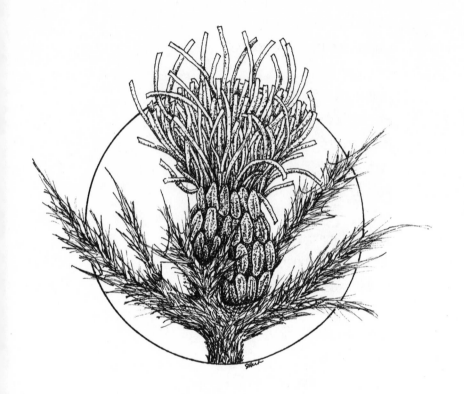

How I love it
when what I've known
as a weed
in me
suddenly becomes
a beautiful flower.

How I delight
when the rejected part
of me
becomes my friend.

How I cherish
the struggles
that change
my inner enemies
into my beloved friends.

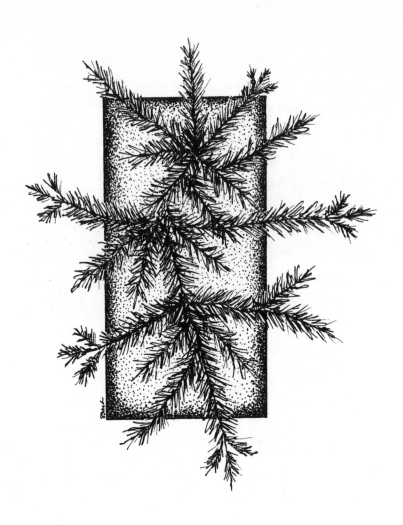

Evergreen trees,
sharp, sturdy needles,
strong to the touch
but often too edgy
to hold without hurt.

The sturdy structure
endures wild winter storms
but the sharpness
keeps away
a touch of comfort.

I wonder now
what kind of needles
protrude from my spirit,

which ones protect
and ward off danger,

which ones
sharply keep others
away.

To stand apart,
to stand out
from the others.

Being different
is exhilarating.
Being different
can also taste
of loneliness.

Growth comes
in strange spurts
and propels us
on our way.

What can we do
when we grow up
and out, too far
on the edge,

except to rejoice
in our uniqueness?

When I was
but a babe
in my spiritual growth,
I followed closely
the wise ones,
the mentors,
the visionaries.

Now that I have grown
I still need mentors,
wise ones,
and visionaries.

Only now
we swim side by side.

Now I trust
my own path,
as well as
the path of others.

Standing tall,
rising up with glory,
doesn't just happen.

All that strength,
all that courage,
began with littleness.

A tiny seed
believing it could grow,
willing to risk
the journey to strength.

One heart-shaped pink pod
falls from the branch,
returning to the soil
from whence it came.

Even the most beautiful
must fall, fade, return;
all fruit succumbs,
all flowers yield.

When my time comes
to drop from the stem
and return to the Source,
may my tumbling
toward the One
be a dance of surrender.

Let me fall
into rebirth
with wonder.

dreams of

inner freedom

April rains are welcomed
by the thawing winter soil,
almost overnight
the grasses grow green.

They have waited for this moment.

Now everything in them
pushes up and outward
toward the light,
seeking the freedom of growth
liked a caged one caught,
finally sprung loose from captivity.

The caged ones within me
are also breaking free.
They are singing spring songs
and dancing in the rain.

Spiritual wings
fly uncluttered,
letting go
of the safe base,
trusting open space,
believing in another
place to land,
one that will hold me
in nurturing embrace.

Inner freedom.

My wings grow stronger
with every flight.

I am no longer
quite so deceived
by the shadows
of my life.

It is painful
to come out
into the open.

Even though the sun
is magnificent
in warmth,
I can hardly
bear its light.

Yet, I've lived
beneath toadstools
and under shrubbery
far too long.

It is time
to stand strong,
to welcome
bright sunbeams.

Will I live my life
always in fear
that some distant enemy
might invade my space
and cause me pain?

Or will I choose
instead
to celebrate
what I now have,
with its quiet beauty
and unfettered joy?

I notice
how some trees
have a storm-swept
personality.

Growing bent,
curled, or misshapen,
no straight up
for them.

Strength shows
through their shapes
of suffering,
sturdy, resilient
in unpretentious forms.

Suffering breathes
into unexpected form,
gives direction, turns us
toward deeper things.

If only I would be
more patient
with the chrysalis
in me,
there could be
beautiful things
coming to life.

I wonder
what keeps me running
from dormancy,
trying to leap
into a butterfly
long before it's ripe,

thus destroying
what could have been
so beautiful.

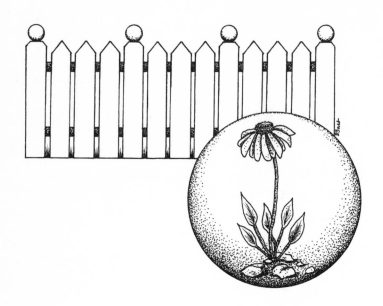

I'm grateful
for simple wildflowers,
renegades of beauty,
paying no heed
to the proper place,
or the acceptable way
to rise up in glory.

Their seeds fall
into waiting earth
with a passionate embrace.

No fenced boundaries,
no limits on their joy,
savoring sun and rain
they root and grow,
singing in the breeze,
content and free.

Oh, wildflowers,
grow and sing inside of me!

Why is it
there are some creatures
I cannot befriend,
like wasps, cockroaches
and skinny red worms
that wriggle too much?

Why is it
that swans, antelope
and frisky white rabbits
have much more appeal?

Why is it
that I cannot befriend
some creatures of my spirit,
like anger, sadness and grief,
while I give an eager welcome
to my visitors
of contentment and joy?

My ego still wears
blinders.
My vision of life
still weeps
with false judgments.

I gaze at their
colored beauty,
admire
their sleek freedom,
entirely forgetting
their dark passage
in the tomb-like
chrysalis.

Butterflies,
wise creatures
of transformation,
remind me
that freedom
doesn't come easily.

I'm thinking
the wings of my self
still have
caterpillar feet.

Thin stems of legs,
delicate sticks,
seemingly fragile,
how deceptive
my view can be.

These wee limbs
provide mobility,
quickness, agility.

And so in my life,
what I see as fragile,
weak and frail,
may be my greatest gift.

Resting
on a narrow leaf-blade,
sharpening perception,
maintaining balance,
all this
and more
before I risk
another giant leap
into the unknown.

There's a part
of me
that belongs
to wide open spaces.

There's a part
of me
that flies
in the vast heavens.

There's a part
of me
that nests
in the woods
and sings
in the trees.

This part
of me
can never be contained
under
a wooden roof.

A new creature
freshly birthed,
feathers still wet,
limbs too weak
to carry it far.

When words
fall onto the page
for the first time,
they taste
newly hatched.

While I wait
for the feathers
to dry,
I dream of the creature,
fully formed,
with strong wings
and robust limbs
that carry far.

Wild rose,
yet hardly wild,
delicate blossoms,
tender leaves,
tiny thorns.

Why so wild?

Only that you grow
free and uncontained,
blooming
in the quiet corners
of countryside
and the open fields
of splendor.

Unhampered
in pastures
of your own choosing,
free to be true
to your wildness.

I long for that much
freedom.

There's a bluebird
in my soul
seeking wings,
longing
for the freedom
to fly
in new, untried
meadows.

She stretches her security
as the passion
to follow whispered
dreams
stirs within her.

Why then
is she still sitting
on the meadow fence?

Fly, bluebird, fly!

There are still
too many
porcupine quills
in me.

There are still
too many
hasty judgments,
edgy hostilities,
harsh defenses,
and biased opinions.

I need my
protective quills

but I must stop
aiming them
at everyone I fear.

I look to the openness
of trees,
branches spread wide,
receiving,

and I wonder
about the openness
in me,

if my branches
are tightly twined
around myself
or reaching out,
receiving.

It is time I untwined
what I can.
It is time I spread wide
a heart
much in need of
receiving.

The simplicity
of a violet
sings in my soul.

The push
to be productive,
the rush
to be responsible,

all this fades
in the beauty
of the violet.

I struggle again
to be free
from seductive lies
telling me
to crowd my days
with success.

I turn mindfully
to the violet
and kiss her
tenderly.

Fly, fly,
far, deep, long,
you creature
in my soul
who knows more
about freedom
than I do.

Fly, fly,
take me there
where
secrets of the self
wait to be wept,
sung, danced.

Fly, fly,
for I long
for freedom
even as I fight it.

Sometimes I listen long
like a praying mantis
gone "dead" with fear.

I listen for what might harm.
I wait for the sound
of an enemy approaching.
I guard against disaster.

Then again, I listen long
for silent songs
playing in hidden places,
melodies urging me on,
rhythms with passion.

Unfortunately,
I am often in my play-dead pose
when the marching band
of ecstatic rapture
passes by.

My world
always seems
a bit too small,
too snug, too tight,
too confining.

I long
for open spaces,
vastness
that stretches,
landscape
reaching far.

I yearn to be
expansive
and all-embracing.

Someday.

dreams of

p e a c e

Gentle things
sway in the breeze
of my soul.

They do not speak
or call to me,
they simply dance
with tenderness.

Gentle things,
when they dance
I am at peace.

When they sway
in my soul,
all things sad
are transformed.

I need
to be still,
let Earth's beauty
embrace me.

For it is in
this embrace
I come home
to the deepest part
of my true self.

Earth consoles
and heals me.
Earth restores
my waning energy.

Earth calms
my confusions,
straightens
my imbalance.

O Earth,
embrace me!

There are benefits
to being hidden.
I find a safe haven,
contentment, peace,
space to remember,
time for wisdom.

There are drawbacks
to being hidden.
No one finds me,
my view of life
is limited,
the days grow long.

Hiddenness homes
insight and wisdom,
but it also harbors
loneliness.

Here in the green forest
I know a presence
bigger than myself,
stronger than
the ponderosa pines.

Here in the whispering forest
I hear a voice
softer than the sighing
of swaying branches.

Here in the dark forest
I see a truth
shining through the boughs,
telling me
I am not alone.

Tiny forest life,
so insignificant
one easily passes by,
without a nod
or a notice.

The treasures
are there
for those with eyes
looking closely.

As I walk
through my days
how much I miss,
because the eyes
of my heart
are dim and drowsy.

Green sings
like no other
color.

Green rings
my heart round
with the starlight
of laughter,
the dance
of enthusiasm.

Green brings
vibrant shoots
of energy
laced with passion.

Green flings
bouquets of dreams
meant to come true.

Old
gnarled tree,
tiny trace of green
left in dead limbs.

The force
of many winds
wrapped
around her heart.

The drawing power
of many suns
seasoned in her
now dry skin.

Old,
how can old
be so beautiful?

I run around
here and there
scurrying, hurrying,
rushing.
From tree to tree,
I leap and dash.

Would I find
just as much food
if I went more slowly,
looked more calmly?

Would I enjoy my life,
be more delighted,
if I paused and smiled
in going here and there?

Who we are,
how we are,
always touches
into other lives.

We may think
we are alone,
apart, separate,
but not so.

Our positive
(or negative)
energy
connects, unites,
draws
(or repels).

Always we touch
others,
always.

In silence,
in stillness,
your majesty,
your mystery
sails into my soul.

Like the full moon,
lighting all darkness
with her unfurling sails
on a quiet
summer's night.

Time alone
on the lake of life,
just floating along,
waiting,
pondering,
no need to be
anywhere,
no need to do
anything.

Time alone.

Stop the crazy rush,
I say to myself,
and sit awhile
on the lake of life.

Winter birds
have their ways
of survival.

They fluff out
their feathers,
fend off the freeze,
find food
in secret sources.

The winter bird
in me,
she, too, fluffs feathers,
finds food
in a season grown cold
and barren.

Blessed be
that winter bird
in me.

It is good to hide
sometimes.
There is the ripe time
to be tucked away
amidst a season's colors,
knowing the only one
who can find me
is myself.

Camouflage time
gives me dreaming space,
helps me discover again
my inner wisdom,
without distractions.

I like
to hide.

So much
of this world
lives in
bigger than,
better than,
more than.

Those who are
small
seem to have
no place
among the strong,
the tall, the sleek.

Yet, each one
has a place
and all is connected.
Each needs
the other
in this compassionate
web
of universe.

Today
joy is looking at me
like I'm the only one
she's attending.

Her radiant smile
and glowing eyes
fall upon my heart,
lifting the heavy gates
in the dark dungeon
of busyness.

A smile of beauty
mixed with radiance,
that's all it takes
to bring me home again
to happiness.

I lift my face,
feel the first touch
of dawn's stunning rays.

They kiss with warmth,
welcome me kindly
after a dark night
of thick thunderstorms.

The wet woods are
wild with the memory
of lightning bolts
and heavy rains.

Slowly the sun's strength
weaves the woods
into silent laughter.

I let go
of memories
wrapped in thunderstorms
and dark nights

and songs of all sorts
form in my heart.

Content we are,
the two of us,
to sit inside
each other's heart.

Glad for the time
to visit our lives
and tell our stories.

We laugh.
We dream.
We sometimes cry.

And always
we listen
with amazement
to the singing
in the other's soul.

The clear call
of the bright red sentinel
of dawn
sweeps out
dreams
from my sleepy mind.

I become aware
of the intense beauty
of life,
the gift of another day.

And while the cardinal
continues to call,
my soul weeps
with the wonder of it all.

In the hurry,
in the rush,
simple things missed,
blessings denied,
beauties ignored.

In the calm,
in the quiet,
simple things received,
mystery unfolds,
happiness blooms.

In the peace,
in the harmony,
I taste with love
all that is good.

Oh, to live near
the roots,
to have a home
close to the heart
of deepest belief.

Oh, to live near
the source,
to sip of the life
that surges
through the veins
of creation.

Oh, to live near
the depths,
to draw strength
from the solid
foundations
of love.

Sometimes
the silence in my soul
is a deafening roar
of anguish
and confusion.

Other times
the silence in my soul
is a soft companion
of love
and comfort.

Yet again
the silence in my soul
is a sturdy sentinel
seeing from afar
wisdom waiting for me.

The tones of my life
are often subdued,
muted with paradox,
dimmed
by internal blindness,
hidden
in the folds
of external activity.

Ssshhh,
I hear them calling
in my mind's eye,
calling, calling,
hazily revealing
a place I long to be.

It is none other
than the heart
of Mystery,
the dwelling place
of Home.

A Note From the Artist

Art, to me, is life-giving. The opportunity to illustrate these poems has been a great gift over the past two years, a joy-filled part of my life journey. Joyce Rupp came to me at a time when my life took an unexpected and difficult turn. She offered me hope and then, with her poems, helped bring those hopes to fruition.

Pondering these nature-based, introspective poems, I found them to be eloquent in their simplicity, centered in creation and humanness, provoking growth and prayer. So true to life, the poems called for realistic rendering and led to hours of delightful research. What marvelous variety surrounds and abounds in our world! God's creation is a vivid, vital gift, a feast for our senses and our souls. To convey this in word and/or image is both a privilege and a pleasure.

What an inspiration the poems have been to me as I tried to portray their essence in pen and ink. At first, the number of illustrations seemed daunting. That feeling faded and each rendering became an absorbing challenge. Each challenge became a small, energizing reward of its own as the images came to life. I hope I have captured the essence of the poems and I hope, too, that all who peruse this book will experience with me the joy I find and feel in God's wonder-full gifts of nature, art, and life.

Barb Loomis

Books by Joyce Rupp

Fresh Bread

Praying Our Goodbyes

The Star in My Heart

May I Have This Dance?

Little Pieces of Light

Dear Heart, Come Home

The Cup of Our Life

Your Sorrow Is My Sorrow

May I Walk You Home?
   (co-authored with Joyce Hutchison)

Prayers to Sophia

Out of the Ordinary

Inviting God In

The Cosmic Dance

Joyce Rupp is well known for her work as a writer, spiritual "midwife," and retreat and conference speaker. A member of the Servite (Servants of Mary) community, she has led retreats throughout North America, as well as in Europe, Asia, Africa, and Australia. Joyce is the author of numerous books, including the best-sellers *The Cup of Our Life*, *Out of the Ordinary*, and *The Cosmic Dance*.

Barbara Loomis is likewise a member of the Servite community. Having taught both grade and high school and been involved in community service, she is now a full-time free-lance and community artist. Barbara exhibits her work and has been the recipient of several awards.

More books by Joyce Rupp...

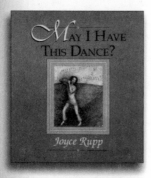

May I Have This Dance?
Prayer is a dance with the Divine. Joyce
Rupp shows you how to let God lead.
ISBN: 0-87793-480-0 / $12.95

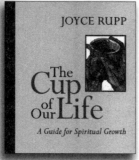

The Cup of Our Life
A Guide for Spiritual Growth
The humble cup, also a rich symbol of
our lives, a sacred vessel that can
connect us with God.
ISBN: 0-87793-625-0 / $12.95

Fresh Bread
And Other Gifts
of Spiritual Nourishment
This handbook for spiritual growth helps
us find the touch of God in common
events, places, and objects throughout
the year.
ISBN: 0-87793-283-2 / $10.95

Prices subject to change